Divine Assignment

Discovering Your Purpose, Destiny, and Triumph through the Trials of Life

BISHOP A.L. HOLLEY

(A Division of D.L. Gilbert Ministries)
www.DLGilbert.org
(754) 333-1-**DLG**

Scripture quotations taken from both the King James Version Bible.

Cover design by Dr. D.L. Gilbert

ISBN-13: 9798278388975

Foreword

by: Dr. D. L. Gilbert

Greetings, in the name of our Lord and Savior: JESUS CHRIST! I am Dr. D.L. Gilbert, Music Producer, Presiding Bishop of New Revelation Global Church, and fellow Author. It is my passion to equip the Body of Christ through the communication of writing and publication. I am honored to bring you this Forward to this awesome work.

Thus, I need you to know that here are moments in life when Heaven interrupts the ordinary rhythm of our days with a divine summons—an unshakable awareness that God is calling us deeper, higher, and forward. For many, that prompting comes softly, like a whisper. For others, it arrives through the sudden storms of adversity.

But for all of us, purpose is not discovered by accident; it is revealed through intentional pursuit, surrendered obedience, and the refining work of God's hand. It is my belief that this book you now hold was born from such a journey.

I have witnessed, in my own life and in the lives of countless Believers, that God never wastes a wound and never wastes a season. Every trial carries instruction. Every delay contains development. Every valley is pregnant with a victory waiting to be born.

Yet too often, we misunderstand the process. We fear the trial, resist the transition, and therefore miss the triumph that God had already written into our destiny.

DIVINE ASSIGNMENT is more than a book—it is a roadmap. It is a prophetic guide for anyone who has ever wrestled with the weight of calling, the pain of preparation, or the mystery of God's timing.

I believe that within these pages, you will find clarity where there has been confusion, courage where there has been hesitation, and conviction where there has been uncertainty.

My prayer is that as you read, the Holy Spirit will illuminate the specific assignment He has crafted for your life—a purpose ordained before the foundation of the world.

Understand that too many of God's people die full. They leave dreams unbirthed, callings unaccepted, and destinies unexplored. Heaven did not design you for a life of wandering, but for a life of meaning.

You were created intentionally, uniquely, and powerfully for a purpose only you can fulfill. And everything you have endured—every heartbreak, every setback, every night of questioning—has been woven into the fabric of that purpose.

As you journey through the chapters ahead, I want to personally challenge you to do three things:

1. **Open your heart to healing.**

   Some pages may touch tender places, not to expose your wounds, but to show you how God uses them.

2. **Open your mind to revelation.**

   The principles shared here are Biblical, practical, and transformational.

3. **Open your spirit to assignment.**

   God is not merely writing another chapter of your life; He is inviting you into the masterpiece of His will.

It is now my honor and joy to turn this over to my fellow co-laborer in the Kingdom, Bishop A.L. Holley, to guide you through this exploration of Divine Trials, Transition, and Triumph.

May this book awaken what has been dormant, ignite what has grown dim, and confirm what God has already whispered to your soul.

Your destiny is calling. Your assignment is waiting. Your triumph is assured.

Now, walk with the man of God through this journey—step by step, truth by truth, revelation by revelation—until you stand confidently in the fullness of the Divine Assignment God has prepared for you.

Table of Contents:

Introduction

Introduction

My dear friend, if you are holding this book, chances are you are standing at a crossroads—one of those sacred intersections in life where the familiar feels uncomfortable, and the future feels uncertain. Perhaps something inside you has been stirring, quietly but persistently, like a whisper you can't shake.

You feel the ache of a calling you can't quite name, a pull toward something greater, something beyond your current understanding. Maybe you look at your life and wonder, "IS THIS ALL THERE IS? SURELY THERE MUST BE MORE THAN THE ROUTINE, MORE THAN THE SURVIVAL, MORE THAN THE QUESTIONS."

Or maybe your crossroads is not internal but circumstantial. Maybe you are reeling from a sudden blow—a loss you didn't expect, a tragedy you didn't foresee, a betrayal you didn't deserve, or a failure that shook you to your core.

Sometimes it is the storm, not the whisper, that awakens us. Perhaps you are here because everything familiar has been disrupted, and you are left holding the fragments of a life you no longer recognize, asking the most painful question of all: WHY?

If that is you, hear me clearly: **you are not alone.** Every soul that has ever walked the earth has wrestled with the mystery of purpose. We are not designed merely to exist—we are designed to MATTER.

Something within us aches for significance, for direction, for meaning. We measure our days not by time but by purpose. We long to know that our journey has reason, that our tears have value, that our struggles are not wasted.

And so, this book—these words—are not meant to entertain you, distract you, or offer a quick spiritual remedy. **This is not a self-help manual promising five easy steps to success.**

Life is far more complex, and God's process far more sacred, than formulas and motivational slogans can contain. What you are holding is an invitation. A journey. A map into the heart of God's design for your life.

This is a journey into the heart of God's plan—a plan that has been operating in your life long before you had the language to describe it. His plan is often hidden in plain sight, veiled not in mystery but in the very experiences you've walked through.

It is wrapped in the unexpected, shaped through seasons of discomfort, and revealed through moments that felt more like breaking than becoming. But here is the truth that will anchor every chapter of this book: **Your life is not an accident. Your suffering is not random.** You were created intentionally—crafted with precision, marked by purpose, and set apart for a specific assignment—A DIVINE ASSIGNMENT.

Everything you have endured, everything you have survived, and everything you are currently navigating is part of the preparation for that assignment. Not one tear, not one setback, not one disappointment has been wasted.

Your story is being written by a God who specializes in transforming pain into purpose, obstacles into open doors, and trials into testimonies.

In the chapters ahead, we will walk together—step by step—through the three phases of discovering, embracing, and fulfilling the assignment God has placed upon your life:

1. Divine Trials

Were we learn that suffering is not punishment, but preparation; a holy forging that shapes the vessel for its future purpose.

2. Divine Transition

Where God moves us from the weight of preparation into the readiness of purpose, shifting our mindset, strengthening our spirit, and aligning our direction.

3. Divine Triumph

Where we step boldly into our calling, living out the reason we were created and recognizing the victory that God has already established on our behalf.

So I invite you now—prepare your heart. Prepare your mind. Prepare your spirit. Let the simple but powerful truths contained within these pages speak peace to your confusion, purpose to your pain, clarity to your crossroads, and strength to your weariness.

This is your moment of divine discovery. It is time—past time—to uncover the assignment placed upon your life before the foundation of the world. Your journey begins now.

Chapter One

Divine Trials

The Uncomfortable Truth
About Purpose and Pain

To begin our journey toward discovering your Divine Assignment, we must start in the place most people avoid: the difficult, painful seasons of life. The world wants us to believe that a life of purpose is a life free of struggle.

We see images of successful people and assume their journey was smooth, their victories instantaneous. This is a profound lie.

In God's economy, the greatest assignments are always preceded by the greatest trials. If you are struggling right now—if you feel broken, confused, or like you've been sidelined by tragedy—then you are exactly where God refines His most precious vessels.

The Problem of the Tragic *'Why?'*

When tragedy strikes, we often instinctively cry out, "Why me?" This is a natural human response, but it is a question that, if left unanswered or misanswered, can derail your entire destiny. The "Why" of suffering is arguably the largest stumbling block to recognizing a Divine Assignment.

People assume that goodness equals ease, and struggle equals abandonment. But the Bible, our firm foundation, tells a different story. Look at Joseph. He was given a magnificent destiny, visions of leadership and authority. But his path to the palace was paved with betrayal, slavery, and false imprisonment.

If Joseph had judged his purpose based on his circumstances in the pit or the prison, he would have concluded that God had forgotten him entirely. God was using the pit not to punish Joseph, but to prepare him.

The pit established humility. The prison taught him patience and administrative skills in isolation. These were essential components of the Pharaoh's Prime Minister, components Joseph could never have learned in the comfort of his father's house.

The trials you face are not random acts of cosmic malice. They are precision tools in the hands of a loving Father.

"My brethren, count it all joy when ye fall into divers temptations; Knowing this, that the trying of your faith worketh patience." (James 1:2-3, KJV)

The word "temptations" here can often be translated as trials or tests. God is telling us to change our perspective entirely.

Instead of viewing a setback as a catastrophe, view it as an opportunity for character development. This is the bedrock of understanding Divine Trials.

The Furnace of Preparation

Imagine a metalsmith preparing to forge a masterpiece. Does he use cold, untouched ore? No. He subjects the metal to the intense heat of the furnace.

Why? To burn away the impurities (the dross) and to make the metal malleable and strong enough to withstand the stress of its final shape.

You, my friend, are the masterpiece. Your trials are the furnace.

What is the dross that God is burning away in your life right now?

•Pride might be burned away by humiliation.

•Self-reliance might be burned away by situations that demand impossible faith.

•Impatience might be burned away in seasons of agonizing waiting.

•Fear might be burned away by facing things you thought you could never survive.

The gold that remains after the fire is pure, beautiful, and valuable. It is ready for the Master's touch.

"That the trial of your faith, being much more precious than of gold that perisheth, though it be tried with fire, might be found unto praise and honour and glory at the appearing of Jesus Christ." (1 Peter 1:7, KJV)

Your faith is more precious than gold. God values the finished assignment so much that He allows the intense heat required to mold you into the person capable of carrying it out. If the assignment is colossal, the preparation must be comprehensive.

The Myth of the Easy Road

We often criticize ourselves because we feel weak or broken during a trial. We think, "If I were truly called, this wouldn't be so hard."

But look at the heroes of the faith. Moses was a murderer who spent forty years hidden in the desert tending sheep before he could lead millions of people.

David was persecuted relentlessly by Saul after he was anointed king. He lived in caves and suffered deep depression and fear.

These were not easy roads. These were Divine Trials designed to ensure that when they finally stepped into their assignment, they knew exactly where their strength came from—not from themselves, but from the Almighty.

The Trials Build Empathy

One profound reason for suffering is that it builds the muscle of empathy necessary for pastoral leadership.

How can you comfort someone who has lost everything if you have never experienced significant loss? How can you counsel someone suffering from betrayal if you have never been betrayed?

Your greatest wounds, once healed, become your most powerful tools of ministry. Your tragedy is not a full stop; it is the introduction to your powerful testimony.

Why Sometimes the Trial Lasts So Long

Sometimes, the trial feels endless. We prayed, we fasted, we waited—and still, the painful situation persists. Why the delay? The delay often relates to the depth of the inner transformation required.

An assignment that affects many people requires a leader whose character is immovable.

Consider the construction of a skyscraper. The deeper and taller the building, the more time and expense must be spent on the foundation. Nobody sees the foundation when the building is finished, but without it, the whole structure collapses.

Your time in the trial is the time God is setting your spiritual foundation. He is rooting out selfishness, reinforcing integrity, and ensuring that you prioritize His voice above all others. This work cannot be rushed.

"The steps of a good man are ordered by the Lord: and he delighteth in his way. Though he fall, he shall not be utterly cast down: for the Lord upholdeth him with his hand." (Psalm 37:23-24, KJV)

Even when you fall during a trial, God's hand is underneath you. He is directing the process. Trust the timing of the Almighty Architect.

Releasing the Victim Mentality

To move from Trial to Transition, we must consciously discard the victim mentality. A victim believes that life happens to them; a person grasping their Divine Assignment understands that life is happening for them, even the difficult parts.

A victim sees their scars and cries about the pain; a visionary sees their scars and celebrates the story of survival.

This subtle shift in perspective—from "Why did this happen to me?" to "What must I learn from this?"—is the gateway to discovering your assignment. It stops the cycle of despair and initiates the cycle of learning and growth.

Your challenge is not to deny the pain. The challenge is to hold the pain in one hand and the promise of Romans 8 in the other:

"And we know that all things work together for good to them that love God, to them who are called according to his purpose." (Romans 8:28, KJV)

Notice the verse does not say all things are good. Sickness, loss, and betrayal are not good things. But God promises that He is powerful enough to orchestrate the outcome so that all things work together for your ultimate good and the fulfilling of His purpose in your life.

This means your divorce, your bankruptcy, your medical diagnosis, the betrayal by a friend—these moments are being woven into the grand tapestry of your destiny. They are foundational blocks for the platform from which you will launch your Divine Assignment.

Practical Steps in the Furnace:

1.Refuse the Lie of Abandonment:

Every day, deliberately speak the truth that God is with you, even if you can't feel Him. He promised He's never leave you.

2.Document the Lessons:

Keep a journal of what you are learning during the trial. What character flaws are being exposed? What new strength are you discovering? This documentation will become the curriculum for those you mentor later.

3.Practice Gratitude:

Gratitude is the spiritual antidote to despair. Find one small thing to thank God for each morning. This keeps your spirit soft and your heart open to His instruction, rather than hardening in bitterness.

4.Seek Shelter in the Word:

The KJV Scriptures are your bedrock. When confusion reigns, cling to the Psalms. When fear grips you, remember the promises of the Prophets. The Word is the anchor that holds you steady in the storm.

Divine Trials are not the end of your story; they are the necessary, powerful beginning of your true calling. Embrace the shaping process. The Master is still working.

Practical

Application

Divine Trials: Walking Through the Furnace With Purpose

Understanding your trials is only the beginning—living through them with clarity, intention, and spiritual resilience is where transformation takes place.

These practical steps will help you navigate the refining seasons of life with wisdom and strength.

1. Acknowledge the Reality of the Trial

Do not hide from the pain or pretend it doesn't exist. Bring it to God honestly.

Prayer:

"Lord, show me what You want me to learn in this season."

2. Reframe the "Why Me?" Question

Instead of asking WHY IS THIS HAPPENING TO ME? Ask: **"What are You forming in me through this?"**

This one shift will reshape your entire perspective.

3. Keep a Refinement Journal

Document:

• What God is teaching you

• Moments of weakness

• Moments of breakthrough

• Scriptures that encourage you

This will later become a blueprint to help others.

4. Build a Scripture Fortress

Choose 3–5 verses and declare them daily.

Examples:

- JAMES 1:2–4

- ROMANS 8:18

- PSALM 34:17–19

Let the Word become your anchor.

5. Identify the Dross

Ask:

"What attitudes, fears, or patterns are being burned away in this fire?" Write down what God reveals: pride, anxiety, control, bitterness, self-reliance, impatience. Then surrender each one intentionally.

6. Actively Reject the Spirit of Abandonment

Trials often "feel" like God has left you. Combat that feeling with truth:

"I will never leave thee, nor forsake thee." **(Hebrews 13:5, KJV)**

Declare it until your emotions submit.

7. Cultivate Daily Habits of Gratitude

Gratitude softens the heart. Write down one thing each day that God sustained you through.

8. Seek Support and Intercession

Do not walk through trials alone. Reach out to your pastor, mentor, or trusted Believer. Their faith can carry you when your faith feels weak.

9. Practice Micro-Obedience

In trials, the Holy Spirit often leads through small instructions. Obey quickly—these small obediences unlock major deliverance.

10. Revisit Past Victories

Recall previous trials God carried you through. This strengthens your present endurance.

Chapter Two

Divine Transition

Moving from
the Wilderness to the Commission

If Chapter One showed us that our trials are preparation, Chapter Two must focus on the crucial step of movement: the **Divine Transition**. This is the stage where the purified soul, having survived the furnace, starts to seek clarity on the actual assignment.

This transition is often the longest, most confusing, and most frustrating part of the journey. It is easy to be brave when the fire is hot (survival mode). It is joyful to celebrate the triumph (receiving the reward).

But the middle ground—the long, silent process of waiting, learning, and character building—is where most people lose heart. This is because the season in your life has just changed.

This is the season of the wilderness.

Let me first say that the wilderness is a school. It's not a waiting room.

When the Israelites left Egypt, they expected a quick trip to the Promised Land. Instead, they got forty years in the desert. Why? Because you cannot take slaves into a promised land; they must first learn to be free people.

The wilderness is where God strips away the dependencies, the former identities, and the worldly comforts that would prevent you from fulfilling your assignment. It is a school for dependence on God alone.

If you feel like you are in a holding pattern —seeking direction, applying for jobs that don't materialize, struggling to launch a ministry that seems stuck—you are likely in your wilderness transition.

Two Key Elements of the Wilderness Transition:

1.Silence and Specific Instruction:

God often speaks loudest in the quiet. When the noise of the trial dies down, we must listen for the specific, detailed instructions for the next steps.

Elijah found God not in the powerful wind, the earthquake, or the fire, but in the "still small voice" (1 Kings 19:11-12, KJV).

2.Developing New Skills:

Your previous life prepared you for survival; your transition prepares you for success. Moses learned management skills from Jethro in the desert. David learned warfare and leadership while fleeing Saul in the caves.

What new skills, spiritual or practical, are you being prompted to develop right now? Do you need to learn patience? Financial management? Better communication? The Divine Transition is time for intentional preparation, not passive waiting.

Unpacking Your Gifts: The Assignment Blueprint

Your Divine Assignment is never something that requires you to become an entirely different person. It is always rooted in the unique way God wired you, combining your natural talents, your spiritual gifts, and the deep lessons learned through your trials.

Think of the parable of the talents (Matthew 25:14-30, KJV). Each servant was given money (talents) according to his ability. God never asks you to do something you are fundamentally incapable of doing. He only asks you to steward the gifts He has already placed within you.

The Three Components of Your Assignment Blueprint:

1. Your Natural Inclinations (Talents):

What do you do well without having to try? Are you a gifted communicator, organizer, encourager, or creator? These are the foundational tools.

2. Your Spiritual Gifts (Authority):

What specific supernatural abilities has the Holy Spirit given you (knowledge, wisdom, healing, service, etc.)? These provide the power for the assignment.

3. Your Scars (Testimony):

What did you survive? This provides the relatability and the authority to speak into the lives of others who are where you once were.

Your assignment is the intersection of these three things. For example, a person with a natural gift for finance (Talent), a spiritual gift of wisdom (Authority), and a history of debt and poverty (Testimony) is powerfully equipped to teach financial stewardship to others who are struggling.

Stop comparing your gifts to others. The assignment God gave the farmer is different from the assignment He gave the fisherman. Both are equally valuable in the Kingdom.

"Having then gifts differing according to the grace that is given to us, whether prophecy, let us prophesy according to the proportion of faith; Or ministry, let us wait on our ministering: or he that teacheth, on teaching..." (Romans 12:6-7, KJV)

The Battle Against Comparison

The transition phase is fraught with the danger of comparison. We measure our progress against the people who seem to have hit their stride faster than us. This is a trap!

Comparison steals your joy and blinds you to the unique preparation God is doing in your life. If God is delaying your launch, it is because the weight of your assignment requires more foundational strength. Your story is unique. Your timeline is divine.

Practical Exercise in Transition:

Spend intimate time with the Lord asking: "Lord, what is it that I know and have endured that qualifies me to help others who are going through the same thing?"

Your assignment is often found in the answer to the problem you have personally faced and overcome.

The Discipline of Alignment and Surrender

Many people mistake the Divine Transition for a season of stagnation when it is truly a season of **alignment**. We often rush forward in our own strength, trying to "make" the assignment happen, only to find ourselves blocked at every turn.

The transition demands surrender. Surrender is not throwing up your hands in defeat; it is placing your hands in the hand of the Father and saying, "You lead."

"Trust in the Lord with all thine heart; and lean not unto thine own understanding. In all thy ways acknowledge him, and he shall direct thy paths." (Proverbs 3:5-6, KJV)

This is the GPS for your destiny. We like to lean on our own understanding—our logic, our resume, our connections. But God's paths are often illogical from a human perspective.

Surrendering means accepting that God's plan, even via the convoluted route, is infinitely better than your quick fix.

How to Maintain Alignment in Transition:

1.Prioritize the Stillness:

Establish a daily routine of quiet time where the goal is not to talk, but to listen. This is where you receive your marching orders.

2.Act on the Small Things:

God rarely reveals the entire scope of the assignment at once. He gives you the next step.

If your assignment involves large-scale leadership, He might first ask you to simply lead a small prayer group or volunteer at a local charity. Faithfulness in the small assignment opens the door to the large one.

3.Covenant with Patience:

Patience is not about waiting; it is about how you wait. It is active endurance. We must actively develop patience, knowing that the timing of the transition is perfecting the result.

"But they that wait upon the Lord shall renew their strength; they shall mount up with wings as eagles; they shall run, and not be weary; and they shall walk, and not faint." (Isaiah 40:31, KJV) Waiting is a spiritual investment that yields renewed strength.

Addressing Fear and Feeling Unqualified

As you move out of the trials and start to glimpse the scope of your assignment, a powerful enemy often emerges: the fear of inadequacy. "Who am I to do this?" "I don't have the education, the funds, or the connections."

This is a classic trap. Every great Biblical figure felt unqualified. Moses stammered. Jeremiah felt too young. Paul felt unworthy because of his past. God is not looking for qualified people; He is looking for available and obedient people. He qualifies those He calls.

When fear suggests you are unqualified, remember this truth: **Your preparation (your Divine Trials) has equipped you perfectly for the people only you can reach.**

Your assignment might be to speak to people who are currently in the exact trial you just survived. Because you lived through it, you have credibility others lack. You are not a motivational speaker; you are a living witness.

The Role of Mentors and Accountability

The transition is too important to navigate alone. God uses other people—mentors, counselors, and spiritual authorities—to confirm your direction and provide correction.

In the Bible, assignments were often confirmed through others: Barnabas affirmed Paul. Eli instructed Samuel. Jethro guided Moses.

If you don't have a spiritual mentor or a trusted community, pray for one. God uses the wise counsel of many to chart the course of your assignment. They can see the forest when you are stuck looking at the trees.

The transition requires humility—the willingness to receive instruction and correction from those assigned to your life. The sooner you embrace accountability, the sooner you leave the wilderness behind.

The End of the Transition

The Divine Transition concludes not when you feel ready, but when God shifts the atmosphere around you. You will know the transition is ending because three things will eventually begin to manifest in your life.

1.Clarity Emerges:

Vague ideas crystallize into distinct steps.

2.Doors Open:

Opportunities, resources, and connections appear effortlessly.

3.Peace Prevails:

The internal struggle and frustration about when are replaced by a deep peace about now.

The final act of the transition is simply stepping out in faith. The Trial prepared your character; the Transition prepared your methodology; now it is time to engage the world with your unique, divinely engineered purpose.

Practical

Application

Divine Transition: Living Wisely in the Wilderness

Transition is not a pause — it is preparation, recalibration, and alignment. These steps help you steward your transition season with purpose and clarity.

1. Establish a Daily Stillness Routine

Set aside 10-20 minutes each day for quiet listening. No requests—just receiving. Record what God whispers.

2. Complete Your Assignment Blueprint

1. **Natural Gifts** (what comes easy)

2. **Spiritual Gifts** (what God empowers)

3. **Scars/Testimonies** (what you survived)

Where these overlap is the core of your calling.

3. Move in Small but Steady Steps

Ask God: "What is the NEXT step You want me to take?" Then take it—no matter how small it may appear.

4. Break the Chains of Comparison

Limit exposure to things that fuel envy. Declare: "My timeline is divine. My path is unique."

5. Develop New Skills Intentionally

Ask: "What do I need to learn for my next season?" Then enroll, study, practice, or seek mentorship.

6. Strengthen Your Spiritual Foundations

Transition is your time to prepare.

Ways to prepare yourself:

- Deepen prayer

- Study Scripture consistently

- Build financial discipline

- Repair or strengthen relationships

- Form accountability partnerships

These will sustain your assignment later.

7. Address the Fear of Inadequacy

Write down every fear. Counter each one with Scripture:

- JEREMIAH 1:5

- EPHESIANS 2:10

- ISAIAH 41:10

Declare, "God qualifies me."

8. Evaluate Your Circle

Ask: "Who pushes me closer to God? Who pulls me away?" Prune accordingly. Some people cannot go where you are going.

9. Practice Surrender Daily

Pray:

"Lord, I surrender my understanding and embrace Your direction." Surrender shortens the wilderness.

10. Watch for the Three Signs Transition Is Ending

1. **Clarity**

2. **Open Doors**

3. **Supernatural Peace**

Once these converge, you are standing at the doorway of assignment.

Chapter Three

Divine Triumph

Living the Assignment and
Claiming Your Victory

We have moved through the fire of the **Divine Trials** (preparation) and navigated the long, instructional season of **Divine Transition** (alignment). Now we arrive at the exhilarating destination: **Divine Triumph**.

Triumph in the context of a Divine Assignment is often misunderstood. We tend to associate triumph with public recognition, wealth, or large-scale fame.

While God may certainly bless your assignment with visibility, true triumph is defined by something far more fundamental: **obedience and completion.**

The greatest triumph is hearing the words of the Master: **"Well done, thou good and faithful servant" (Matthew 25:21, KJV).**

Redefining Triumph:
Obedience Over Outcome

Your assignment is entirely successful if you execute the plan God laid out for you, regardless of how the world measures the result. Imagine two people called to plant a seed.

- One is called to plant a seed that grows into a massive redwood tree.

- The other is called to plant a small flower that only one person will ever see.

If the first person only plants the seed halfway and stops, they failed the assignment. If the second person plants the small flower in the exact location God intended, they achieved perfect triumph.

The output is God's responsibility. The obedience is yours. Many fail to reach triumph because they stop too soon, or they try to perform someone else's assignment.

**Your victory is tied explicitly
to your unique mandate.**

**"For we are his workmanship, created
in Christ Jesus unto good works, which God
hath before ordained that we should walk in
them." (Ephesians 2:10, KJV)**

You are a custom-designed work of art, and your "good works" (your assignment) were ordained by God specifically for you long before you were born. Triumph is simply walking step-by-step in that ordained path.

The Power of Scars:
Your Platform of Authority

When you step into your assignment—whether it's running a business with integrity, raising godly children, leading a church, or serving the poor—you will inevitably face challenges. People will doubt you, situations will arise that seem too complex, and the enemy will try to intimidate you.

At these moments, remember your past. Your scars are not signs of weakness; they are medals of conquest. The authority you carry in your assignment comes directly from the trials you survived.

If you counsel someone battling addiction, your freedom from that same addiction gives your words weight. If you build a ministry for widows, your experience of loss provides a connection that no textbook can replicate.

When Jesus appeared to Thomas after the resurrection, what did He show him? His hands and His side—His wounds (John 20:25, KJV). The marks of suffering were proof of His identity and the source of His ultimate triumph.

In your assignment, never hide your scars. Let them be the proof that God is a deliverer, a healer, and a redeemer. Your testimony becomes the key that unlocks someone else's freedom.

Practical Endurance:
Finishing the Race

Triumph is not a single event; it is persistent endurance until the task is complete. The Bible often compares the Christian life to a race.

"Wherefore seeing we also are compassed about with so great a cloud of witnesses, let us lay aside every weight, and the sin which doth so easily beset us, and let us run with patience the race that is set before us." (Hebrews 12:1, KJV)

The most common reason people fail their Divine Assignment is not a lack of gifting, but a lack of endurance. They run well for a time, but they weary right before the finish line.

Keys to Persistent Endurance in Your Assignment:

1.Lay Aside the Weight:

What is hindering your run? Is it resentment from the trials? Is it fear of failure?

Is it the desire for approval? Identify the "weight" and deliberately lay it aside.

2.Focus on the Goal (Jesus):

Look at the very next verse: "Looking unto Jesus the author and finisher of our faith" (Hebrews 12:2, KJV).

Keep your eyes fixed on Him, not on the critics, the obstacles, or the exhaustion. He initiated the faith in you, and He will finish it.

3.Run with Patience:

This circles back to Chapter Two. Patience is disciplined endurance. Pace yourself.

Realize that monumental assignments take time. Do not burn out by trying to accomplish a life's work in one year.

The Triumph of Legacy and Impact

One of the great joys of living a Divine Assignment is watching the ripple effect of your obedience through the lives of others. Your triumph is rarely just about you.

If you are faithful to your assignment, you create a legacy that extends far beyond your own life.

Think of Paul, who wrote, **"I have fought a good fight, I have finished my course, I have kept the faith"** (2 Timothy 4:7, KJV).

Paul's triumph was not just that he survived his numerous trials (shipwrecks, beatings, imprisonment), but that he passed the baton to others, notably Timothy, ensuring the work continued.

How do you build legacy in your assignment?

•Mentor:

Intentionally pour everything you learned in the trials and transition into one or two chosen people.

•Document:

Write down the principles and processes you learned. This book is a testament to the power of documenting what God taught you.

•Humility:

Ensure that the success of the assignment points back to God, not to your own brilliance. If the legacy is only about you, it will die with you. If it is about the power of God, it will live forever.

The Divine Reward

God is not a passive employer; He is a generous rewarder. The ultimate triumph includes a reward—both here on earth and eternally.

While we should serve out of love, not just for payment, the Bible is clear that faithfulness brings reward.

"Behold, I come quickly; and my reward is with me, to give every man according as his work shall be." (Revelation 22:12, KJV)

The reward is often perfectly tailored to the assignment and the sacrifice made. If your assignment demanded great sacrifice in isolation and obscurity, your reward might be immense public honor.

If your assignment required immense spiritual warfare, your reward will be deep, abiding peace. But the greatest reward is the crown of righteousness reserved for those who finished the race.

"Henceforth there is laid up for me a crown of righteousness, which the Lord, the righteous judge, shall give me at that day: and not to me only, but unto all them also that love his appearing." (2 Timothy 4:8, KJV)

The triumph is secure. The victory is guaranteed for those who remain faithful to the assignment they were given.

Practical
Application

Divine Triumph: Living Out Your Assignment Daily

Triumph is not the applause of the world—it is consistent obedience to Heaven. Use these steps to maintain momentum as you walk in your Divine Assignment.

1. Redefine Success as Obedience

Ask weekly: "Have I obeyed what God asked of me?" If yes, you have triumphed!

2. Steward Your Scars

List:

• Your major battles and the outcome

• Who you can now minister to as a result

Your scars identify your mission field.

3. Begin Building Legacy Now

Document everything:

- Sermons

- Lessons

- Experiences

- Testimonies

- Principles

- Personal revelations

Your assignment should bless generations.

4. Maintain Consistency Through Small

Examples:

• Weekly prayer focus

• Monthly fasting

• Quarterly reflection retreat

• Daily Scripture meditation

Small disciplines create long-term victory.

5. Conduct a "Weights and Wings" Inventory

Weights: fear, pride, distractions, toxic relationships.

Wings: mentors, Scripture, prayer, discipline, vision.

Then, simply remove all the weights and strengthen all the wings.

6. Cultivate Endurance

Meditate on HEBREWS 12:1–2 weekly. Lay aside anything that slows your spiritual pace.

7. Engage Mentorship

Connect with:

- One mentor (who pours into you)

- One mentee (whom you pour into)

This creates a cycle of continuous growth and legacy.

8. Celebrate Every Step

Acknowledge weekly victories—even the small ones. Heaven celebrates obedience.

9. Anticipate and Resist Opposition

Declare:

"Resistance means progress." The enemy only attacks moving targets.

10. Guard Your Peace

Peace is a sign of alignment. If peace leaves, pause and seek God.

11. Stay Present While Pursuing Future Vision

Dream immensely for the future — but obey completely in the present. Victory is built one faithful step at a time.

Chapter Four

The Heart of the Matter

Stepping Boldly Into Your Divine Assignment

As we arrive at the end of this journey, the message of this book becomes unmistakably clear: your life has purpose, your pain has meaning, and your destiny has been divinely orchestrated by God Himself. Every chapter—from Divine Trials, to Divine Transition, to Divine Triumph—has been designed to illuminate the truth that you were created with intention, equipped with unique gifts, and prepared through every season you have endured.

The path to your assignment is not a straight line; it is a God-crafted process. What you once thought was punishment was actually preparation. What felt like delay was in fact development. What seemed like silence was divine alignment. What looked like defeat was ultimately the setup for triumph.

Your Trials:
The Refining Fire of Purpose

Throughout this journey, you have learned that **Divine Trials** are not signs of God's absence—they are evidence of His investment in you. Trials refine, purify, strengthen, and shape you into a vessel capable of carrying the weight of your assignment.

"That the trial of your faith, being much more precious than of gold that perisheth... might be found unto priase and honour and glory at the appearing of Jesus Christ."

(1 Peter 1:7, KJV)

Every hardship, from betrayal to heartbreak, from loss to confusion, has served as a tool in the hands of a loving Father. Your scars are no longer symbols of tragedy—they are the credentials that qualify you to minister to others.

Your Transition:
The Wilderness Classroom

You also discovered that **Divine Transition** is the season where God aligns your heart, trains your hands, and clarifies your vision.

It is where old identities fall away and new purpose begins to take shape. Transition is not wasted time—it is necessary time.

"Trust in the Lord with all thine heart; and lean not unto thine own understanding... and He shall direct they paths."

(Proverbs 3:5-6, KJV)

This is where gifts, talents, and testimony come together. Where you learn patience, develop new skills, and discern the "still small voice" of God leading you into your next step. Transition forms the blueprint of who you are becoming.

Your Triumph:
Living Out the Assignment

Finally, you stepped into an understanding of **Divine Triumph**, which is not defined by applause or accomplishment, but by OBEDIENCE.

Triumph is hearing the Lord say, "WELL DONE." It is the joy of completing the work God entrusted to your hands and witnessing the ripple effect of your obedience in the lives of others.

"I have fought a good fight, I have finished my course, I have kept the faith."
(2 Timothy 4:7, KJV)

Your triumph comes from endurance, humility, and unwavering devotion to the assignment God authored uniquely for you. The legacy you build will outlive you when you walk faithfully in God's purpose.

A Unified Message:
Purpose in Every Step

As you close these pages, remember this foundational truth: **nothing in your life has been wasted.** God used every season—dark and bright, painful and joyful—as preparation for the destiny He placed inside you.

- Your **suffering** prepared you.

- Your **waiting** aligned you.

- Your **obedience** will establish you.

This journey has brought you to a sacred moment — the moment where your understanding becomes action. It is time to rise, time to walk forward, and time to fulfill the assignment Heaven entrusted to you.

"And we know that all things work together for good to them that love God, to them who are the called according to His purpose." **(Romans 8:28, KJV)**

You are called. You are chosen. You are equipped. You are assigned. Step boldly and fearlessly into your Divine Assignment.

Reflection Prayer

Father, in the name of Jesus, I thank You for every chapter of my life— for the trials that refined me, the transitions that shaped me, and the triumphs that await me. Lord, open my eyes to see my purpose clearly. Open my ears to hear Your voice distinctly. Open my heart to obey You fully. Strengthen me where I am weak, heal me where I am wounded, and empower me where You have called me.

Let every scar become a testimony, every delay become preparation, and every step align with Your will. I surrender my gifts, my story, and my future to You. Order my steps, illuminate my path, and guide me into the fullness of my Divine Assignment. In Jesus' mighty name, I pray.

Amen!

Chapter Five

Study Guide & Workbook

The following Sections are designed to deepen your understanding of the principles presented in DIVINE ASSIGNMENT and guide you into practical, Spirit-led application.

Each Section includes:

- **Reflection Questions**

- **Self-Assessments**

- **Journaling Prompts**

- **Action Steps**

- **Scripture Meditation**

- **Prayer Exercises**

You may simply utilize this part for your own personal devotion, navigating through it at your own pace, or in a small group setting.

SECTION ONE:
Studying Divine Trials

Understanding the Furnace of Preparation

Reflection Questions

1. What trial has most shaped your life in the last five years?

2. How has your view of suffering changed after reading this chapter?

3. What patterns or habits has God exposed during your trials?

4. Which emotions are most difficult for you to surrender in hard times?

Self-Assessment:
Identifying the Refining Areas

Rate each area from 1 (weak) to 5 (strong):

- Trust in God during uncertainty: ___

- Patience in long seasons: ___

- Consistency in prayer: ___

- Managing emotions under pressure: ___

- Ability to discern God's hand in adversity:

___

Journaling Prompts

- Describe a trial you misunderstood at first, but later saw God's purpose in.

- Write about a time you felt abandoned by God. What sustained you?

- Identify the "dross" God is burning away in this season.

Action Steps

1. Begin a "Refinement Journal" this week.

2. Choose three Scriptures to declare each morning.

3. Share your testimony with one trusted Believer.

Scripture Meditation

- 1 Peter 1:7

- James 1:2–4

- Psalm 34:17–19

Prayer Exercise

Write a prayer asking God to reveal the purpose of your current season.

SECTION TWO: Studying Divine Transition

Navigating the Wilderness Season

Reflection Questions

1. What part of transition is hardest for you—waiting, shifting, or obeying?

2. What old identity or mindset do you feel God calling you to release?

3. Which gifts or talents do you sense God highlighting in this season?

4. What relationships support your transition, and which hinder it?

Self-Assessment:
Your Transition Readiness

Rate each area from 1 (weak) to 5 (strong):

- Ability to let go of the familiar: ___

- Discernment: ___

- Willingness to obey without full clarity:

  ___

- Emotional stability: ___

- Ability to hear God's voice in stillness: ___

Journaling Prompts

- Describe a "wilderness" season from your past. What did God teach you?

- Write about a moment when God shifted your direction unexpectedly.

- Reflect on what "obedience" looks like for you right now.

Action Steps

1. Create your ASSIGNMENT BLUEPRINT (gifts, spiritual gifts, scars).

2. Schedule one weekly silent time of listening.

3. Identify one small obedience you can take this week.

Scripture Meditation

- Isaiah 43:19

- Proverbs 3:5-6

- Joshua 1:9

Prayer Exercise

Write a prayer surrendering your timeline and asking God to align your direction.

SECTION THREE:
Studying Divine Triumph

Walking in Victory and Purpose

Reflection Questions

1. What does "triumph" mean to you now?

2. How has God used your scars to help others?

3. What fears arise when you think about stepping fully into your assignment?

4. What legacy do you want your obedience to create?

Self-Assessment: Triumph Lifestyle Checklist

Rate each from 1 (weak) to 5 (strong):

- Consistency in spiritual disciplines: ____

- Courage to obey: ____

- Emotional resilience: ____

- Confidence in your calling: ____

- Willingness to invest in others: ____

Journaling Prompts

- Write about a victory that required great faith.

- Describe how God has transformed your pain into purpose.

- Reflect on the people God may be calling you to mentor.

Action Steps

1. Write out your assignment and place it somewhere visible.

2. Begin weekly progress check-ins.

3. Identify a mentor and a mentee.

Scripture Meditation

- 2 Timothy 4:7

- Romans 8:31–39

- Hebrews 12:1–2

Prayer Exercise

Write a prayer dedicating your gifts, time, and future to God's assignment.

Additional Tools

Monthly Destiny Tracker

- What did God teach me this month?

- What step of obedience did I take?

- Where did I experience resistance?

- What breakthroughs occurred?

- What needs adjustment next month?

Spiritual Growth Habits Checklist

- Daily prayer

- Scripture study

- Weekly fasting (optional)

- Journaling

- Worship time

- Rest & Sabbath discipline

- Accountability check-ins

Prayer & Declaration Pages

Dedicated blank pages for writing your own:

- Declarations of faith

- Monthly prayer goals

- Testimonies

- Praise reports

Final Encouragement

This workbook is not just an accessory—it is a tool of transformation. As you reflect, pray, journal, and take action, you are stepping deeper into your Divine Assignment.

God is shaping you, guiding you, and preparing you to walk boldly into destiny. Continue in faith. Continue in obedience. Continue in purpose. Your assignment is calling — walk in it fully.

Made in the USA
Middletown, DE
18 January 2026

27270535R00064